STILL ANOTHER PELICAN IN THE BREADBOX

Kenneth Patchen

Edited and with an Introduction by

Richard Morgan

PIG IRON PRESS
Youngstown, Ohio

ISBN 0-917530-14-4
Library of Congress Catalogue Card Number 80-82905

Printed in Youngstown, Ohio

PIG IRON PRESS
Post Office Box 237, Youngstown, Ohio 44501

This book is for Miriam

and it is for all the creatures of the world, particularly those who have been brutalized by the barbarism and cruelty of the human race; for every dog and cat now in a city pound, without love or care, awaiting a horrible death; for every animal crushed on the highways or starving in the streets of the world; for every animal tortured in scientific experiments, with no hope of an end to its suffering except a death both painful and unnecessary; for every creature killed to satisfy people's taste for flesh; for all creatures from the smallest to the largest, who have suffered or who are now suffering from human sadism, carelessness, or stupidity.

To them also is this book dedicated

TABLE OF CONTENTS

FOREWORD

It seems almost like a Patchen joke carried to the extreme — the *Pig Iron Press* in *Youngstown, Ohio* is publishing his early and unpublished work. If Kenneth had authorized this publication, his "critics" would surely scorn such as an obvious Patchen ploy. Yet, how appropriate that he go back to "Mr. Youngstown Sheet & Tube" to disprove the words of Thomas Wolfe.

Word that Kenneth's last book will spring to visible life from Youngstown brings back memories of the blast furnaces spitting fire into the black night as we passed through there in 1934 on our way to Warren. Far into many nights Kenneth talked of the blast furnaces and rolling mills. For many, world-wide, Patchen is identified with his Youngstown Sheet & Tube. He wrote it at a time of economic depression. Poverty was an open wound everywhere, and especially in areas of heavy industry. Youngstown was, and is today, the archetype of how economic disaster can destroy all.

Out of this economically and culturally stripped bare area came an individual. He had seen all forms of life hurt, starved, cowed, withered, and sored. "Everything that lives is holy," he said. Everything he said and did all his life — and now and forever — was to try to inculcate that belief in others, whoever, whatever they are.

Extraordinary as it may seem, unlikely as any hope for a future may be, Kenneth always believed, always hoped.
"I believe in the truth.
I believe that every good thought I have
All men shall have.
I believe that what is best in me
Shall be found in every man.
I believe that only the beautiful
Shall survive on the Earth."

Miriam Patchen
Palo Alto, California
1980

INTRODUCTION

There was a man, Kenneth Patchen, who rose from a town of soot and steel to stand before the world. With fury and delight he created kingdoms of magical creatures, landscapes of horror, and simple testaments of personal love. Here before you are his remains: the early, the overlooked, the last.

He was born December 13, 1911, in Niles, Ohio, the third of six children in the family of Wayne Patchen and Eva McQuade. Eva, the daughter of Hugh McQuade, a man of poetic temperament and a reputation for spiritual healing, was a severe, very religious woman who spent her time caring for her children. Wayne, the result of generations of native-born Patchens, held a good position in the Youngstown steel mill.

The family soon moved to Warren, Ohio, where Wayne worked for the mill and, on his own, built houses to sell and rent, while the family migrated from house to house as each dwelling was sold. Patchen's childhood was secure, though not affluent; The houses were just outside the "acceptable" neighborhoods of the town. This was at a time when Warren was becoming a commercial center; grey smoke was starting to envelop the Mahoning river valley where the town was situated, a certain brackishness had crept into the water, and the factory town slums had become a common sight.

Nonetheless, civic pride was in evidence; a large municipal building was erected in the center of the city, and a new town library was constructed with a grant from Andrew Carnegie, in whose industries the citizens labored. Patchen progressed from Frances Willard Elementary School, to East Junior High School, and finally arrived at Warren G. Harding High School in September 1925. His childhood had the qualities of terror and joy common to most: he suffered through the death of his beloved sister Kathleen, and his father's injury in the mill; he enjoyed the Marx brothers, Saturday afternoon opera on the radio, walking through the woods, driving around in the roadster his father had purchased for him, discussing the labor movement and politics with his father and their friends, athletics, and other typical pursuits. He read a great deal, kept a daily journal, and began to form the dreams he would attempt to live out in the coming years.

In school, he was successful but insecure. His intellectual capacities earned him the respect of classmates. He was editor of the school yearbook, *Echoes*, in the year he graduated, and was a prominent figure on the school track team. On April 12, 1928, his first poem, reprinted here for the first time, "The Christ of the Andes," was published in the school newspaper, *High School Life*. All six of the poems that appeared in that periodical between then and May 24, 1929, are included in this collection. While in high school, "Permanence" was accepted for publication in the *New York Times*, though it was not actually printed until 1932. But despite these successes, there were problems. A naturally quiet person, Patchen was very shy and uncertain with women, perhaps a legacy of the strict religious background of his mother, or the lack of interest in such things on the part of his father, but whatever the cause, it was a problem which caused him pain for years to come. He also felt a great need to prove himself, and fought feverishly for election to school offices, in order not to seem merely one of the faceless persons who are a part of any institutional setting. His athletic attainments aside, he was often bothered by physical ailments.

The fall after graduation, he entered the newly-established experimental college at the University of Wisconsin. But the summer between high school and college brought the Depression to the Patchen household. Wayne lost his job in the mill, the houses that had been built were empty, or occupied by people who could not pay rent or mortgages, and Patchen was, from this point on, entirely on his own. Though he made friends there, Patchen was not happy at Wisconsin, and left at the end of the academic year, to begin several years "on the road," moving from place to place, through Arkansas, Louisiana, and Georgia (where in a case of mistaken identity, he was picked up, beaten, and thrown into jail, where he remained for several days). Leaving the south, he roamed through the midwest, Pennsylvania, and New York, finally settling in Boston in 1933. During these years, he wrote the poems "Lenin" and "reversing the Inquest," which were published in the *Rebel Poet*, and the short stories in this collection, none of which were ever published. He became politically aware during his travels, partly through his reading, partly through exposure to life in disadvantaged circumstances, and this awareness took shape in *Before the Brave*, his first book, a celebration of revolutionary transformation and of individual love.

On Christmas Eve 1933, he joined some friends in Boston to see a marionette show and go to a party. Miriam Oikemus, a young girl attending Massachusetts State College, was also at the party, and they met. For Patchen, unemployed, underfed, in despair at the age of twenty-two, the encounter was an emotional collision that forever altered his life. They spent the evening together; the next day, Patchen wrote two poems for her, to be followed by more, and then through the years by books, paintings, creations of every type, each and all dedicated "For Miriam."

Over the next few months, they saw each other as often as possible, while Patchen wrote, picked up work wherever he could, and had his first major publication, in *Poetry*. In May, he and Miriam left Boston, and went to live together in New York. They stayed there a few weeks, and then went to Ohio to visit Patchen's parents. On June 28, 1934, they were married in a simple ceremony, without friend or family, in Sharon, Pennsylvania. Patchen's death in 1972 ended the marriage, after thirty-eight years.

Before the Brave was published by Random House in 1936. Between then and his death, he wrote over forty books of poetry, prose, and drama. In addition, he produced hundreds of individually hand-painted books, and innumerable silkscreen prints, original paintings, papier-mâché animal sculptures, and drawings. He also pioneered the poetry-and-jazz movement, reading his works with noted musicians around the country, and making several recordings in that genre. The critical pieces which are reprinted here are from those intervening years, and none of the articles has been reprinted prior to this. The chronology which begins on page 86 lists the books and the various places Patchen lived before finally settling in Palo Alto in 1956.

The remaining poems, and *Jeremiah Dork* (which is the beginning of what was to be a longer work), appear here for the first time. They were all written during the last ten years of Patchen's life, when he was living in the house on Sierra Court in Palo Alto. The house itself is simple but beautiful, like many of Patchen's poems, particularly those written late in his life. It is decorated with the artifacts of Patchen's mind and heart: sculptures made from the leftover scraps of papers he used in silkscreening, such as a smiling blue bear, and a little yellow bird; his "painted books," with patterns, imaginary creatures, and strange, wonderful people leaping from the covers; poem-paintings, in which word and image are blended to form something which exceeds either; silkscreens; gifts from admirers around the world; and above all else, the gentle touch which Miriam brought to him, and still brings to the house he inhabited. Breezes stir the leaves of trees and bushes they planted in the front yard, and in the back, legions of black squirrels tap on the windowpanes, demanding the walnuts they are accustomed to receiving each day from the people in the house.

But behind the beauty and the love, there was a searing, uncontrollable pain. Beginning with a back injury in the late 1930's, and complicated by botched operations and a deteriorating body, Patchen was helpless in bed for most of the last twenty years of his life; his back was in a state of semi-paralysis, and the disease carried with it fits of depression and moments of unbearable pain. This coupled with the poverty which continued almost unabated throughout his adult life forms the rest of the world which shaped these remaining works.

*   *   *   *

With the publication of this book, virtually all that Patchen wrote and preserved has now been published. *Patchen's Lost Plays* (Santa Barbara: Capra Press), containing the only two plays he wrote, was published five years after his death, in 1977. *The Collected Letters of Kenneth Patchen* (Santa Barbara: Black Sparrow Press) is scheduled for publication next year. A comprehensive work. *Kenneth Patchen, an Annotated, Descriptive Bibliography* (Mamaroneck, NY: Paul Appel), and a critical collection, *Kenneth Patchen: A Collection of Essays* (New York: AMS Press) were published recently. All other books by Patchen are published by New Direction (New York).

I have been doing research and writing on Kenneth Patchen for almost ten years, and the number of people whose assistance should be acknowledged after that long is so large it would fill this book if I but listed their names. Many I have thanked in previous books, and those I have neglected have long since either accepted my apologies or given up on me entirely. So I will limit the acknowledgements to two.

Miriam Patchen has made it possible, and enjoyable, through the years, to do this work. She is a fine woman, and you all should meet her.

And as Patchen had his Miriam, so do I have mine. Lissa Fischer has taught me, through great adversity and times exceedingly lean, that it is most important to love, and to be good to all creatures, and never to give up. She and Momma Cat, much like the black cats of Patchen's life, offer instruction so right and so mystifying that it cannot be ignored. And I thank the creatures they have brought to join our household, R.G., Annie, Marmelade, Ben, Violet and family, Ellie, Martin, Daisy, Shadow, Max, Bunny, Dan, Felicia, Rasputin, Roscoe, Willard, and Big Gray, all who are with me now, and are collectively my reason for this and for every book.

Richard Morgan
Jonesboro, Tennessee
May 1980

STILL ANOTHER PELICAN IN THE BREADBOX

THE STORY OF JEREMIAH DORK
AND THE KILADIAN FOREST

Moved restlessly under the living tree. A sturdy day —
God's things mating and killing in their flowery pain.
Wonder without end.

He moved his fingers against the rough skin. It was
noon. He saw no one in the sky.

Upon a hill two lions went together — screaming in an
agony of joy and despair. Golden ones, beautiful and
cruel.

Natives picked weeds for supper. It looked sad with
their shrunken bodies being so well known to each other.

Then she appeared again, her rump and breasts scarred
as before with the tribal nonsense. Don't touch, gods:
this isn't even hers — it belongs to us. Throw open her legs
and life and let only us in!

As before, their eyes met across the river.

Dork's hand throbbed in its place against the tree.

I am crying inside me. Late watcher — Ras Algethi,
Canes Venatici, Cor — Caroli — giving drink to peaceful
cattle within ordained limits shine forth in glory, O Nile.

19

Khepera ghosts of beginnings and the dead always what is done clutters the world with its dying. Always the seed sprouts in the warm earth.

Festers and damns, the cold flesh of history — An ugly animal, fouled at his holes. Look how in this time Art and Religion are so much toilet-paper they plunk their bloody money down on the counter for like everything else.

THE MOCKING AIR AROUND US

"The captives are brought to the pits mouth. Their arms and legs are now broken with clubs, and they are pushed into the pit on the top of the king's body and those of his wives."

It is dark here. I wish I had somebody good to talk to. My coat is like an ugly skin under my head. Tomorrow is another dying.

Idly my thoughts turn to Helen. Should be safe up here — it was the biggest tree around. O come lend with me and be my lay. A nut-hatcher calls sleepily.

Far below the taxis hoot.

Good night, my soul.

He finds her in his dream, upright as a rosestained quill, not blurred at all. O Under the bewildering — is what answer?

Can one believe when he himself is unworthy of belief. Outside always are the gods.

Awaking

sees the statue crowned with flowers.

Shake it up, Jack.

Eh? Oh, cuppa cawfee — two sugars.

A tale of Greece. (Cold eyes in a silent face.)

Will you hang up and dial again please.

". . . nobody pray." Came in this morning's mail. Herman has left Louise. Why that   dirty little slut! Montana will be completely without grass in another twenty-five years. The good king Colladabad was killed by one crunch of a hippopotamus. Yet less than a percentage of our people believe in a life before taxes. At rest in their grim poverty, are the dead. They nourish now, who were ever unnourished. These poor human things.

Jerry Dork hitches up his pants and clears his wind-canal. With fading interest he watches the blood pouring out of the mouth of the statue.

— Fiery porcupine.

The sun picks the nose of the tower clock. On the quaint little platform of the railway station a gluttonous school-boy is sick. Where am I going? Hell, I've been there.

Only thing of its kind in America — a brother for snakes. Some of them twenty feet long. The pink satin pillows, beaded lamps, *rosebud* and *bluebirds* on the wallpaper — Bless This Our Own Dear Home — something to see however — fifteen miles out of Toledo — slithering cold as a rope of lice — young girls, a little scared none-theless, I thought.

Well, now Mr. Breglemeer, this is a surprise; last I heard of you . . . What? oh, who that it was. Bottoms up, lads — here comes that nice old boot round again.

A spear thuds into the kraal at my elbow. I'd never work for a man like it says about today's paper — putting tadpoles in the mucilage jar! Admiral Did he never dood that — O radiant Prince of Heaven.

bitter ashes stop my tongue

Where is there truth!

An old hag watches me from across the river, and a yellowish spittal trickles down upon her withered chin.

And to believem.

They've stolen Mr. Dork's oviparous daughter — and horrible chicks shake up out of coral seas.

Here is a moment of peace in all the press of a trying day. I've taken off my clothes the better to dwell together as husband and wife you with.

Solongsolongso

I like cosing I like thee

I like the holy one who lives in the dell

A ta ta ta ta tum a tum te ta te

A tuma te tum te ta hurrah hurrah

O God none of thy angels is as beautiful as she

21

Jerry, my brazen, frog-hawking twerp, what pleadeth you! There they all lie, the pinch-assed and the cronies of dull witted whores; sweetening alike corruptions jolly liquid tooth . . . How sayeth it? Revenge is a womb? The Primitive sin — not ours, but His? Eh? Eh!

Only if Stars and Trees and Wrens are guilty, have you any guilt to worry about, my poor sleeping friend.

Man is the only thing to be afraid of.

In lonely houses — at least, an apple; songmaker, stranger . . . carnivorous lamb — violent night hairy night — easy damns it O

Life the Giver

all under the falling calling

                    for peace
                    grace
                    and Mercy
          O let the kind lead the kind

Sorrow, my meek hearts, only sorrow and rot

Sit down and make yourself to hell. From this day, all sickness and poverty and fear are abolished. Hatred will keep a little longer. O and when the

Who *is* that on the balcony?

"An immense din of drums, horns, flageolets, gongs, both small and inferior, mingled with the yells of a really frantic crowd, drown the shrieks of the sufferers, upon whom the earth is shoveled and stamped down by thousands of cruel fanatics, who dance and jump upon the loose mould so as to force it into a compact mass through which the victims of this interesting sacrifice cannot grope their way.

HERE LIES J. FREBERSHAM DORK LATE OF (I had me reasons for leavin Leamis City, you bet . . .) 5 six soaking wet, dark blond hair, In Gaol We Trust tatooed on his aine behind, wouldn't ye ken now.

O the unheeding malice of things. Ah Christ the small flowers sweat in the grass of this devouring land

A man split into everywhere.

Sweet love, the scaly roots push up through one,

Golden tresses. Flat on its belly, the weeping god.

22

the evening waters sla a a a a a Hie! (her sideburn kinsmen come —)

Atlantis, Wines of hands . . . To the dream, gentlemen. To freedom. To our dreaming hearts, where pity and love sleep.

Ah lugs and lassies lie on the purpling heath.

Fragrance of teeth — leopard — held innocence of the deer: a cruel tide running back

through billions of suns and earths

— to 'our' God?

All things must hurt to live. Unavoidably, needfully — Why? Why? Why?

Crowns and refuges

over the bloody hills

across the unmoving river

So each being is shrouded in a greater shadow

No one is here except us chilled.

They've made a circle around her, hopping about like bugs. How can I get over? I yell.

Lustily shouting her name: Helen, Helen babe

— Hel! Oh, Hel! Oh, Helen honey! Hel! Oh, Hel!

They do say some nights the fog, why, it plain folds in like a towel of soft cee-mint — course, now since my old' omen up and left me fer that carnival feller, I kinda just stand round here and sort of watch it flowin in, like — had him a neat shifty pair of dukes, I will say that much for the oily sonofabee

Aye, and how many more "wander frozen, rain-drenched, sad and betrayed"?

Goat tracks into the silence. Tired wee bird, carry you rose-pin ribbons out across the abyss? A sturdy speech, man. The lovely human builders, queens and huntsmen asleep in the ground. I — Dork's me handle, mate — am ready to go 'long' with them.

And I knew that it would come round to me. In that reckless workmanship — smashing up a world now and then, to make another. Stars pin-balling all over high and gone.

Are you one of us, cold sombre moths of the heavens

23

Lighthouse — Watcher — years 1867-1903-1518 — tormented? silent? are you *Now?* are we all one thing? Isn't anywhere here? Aren't we the river the swimmer and the one who thinks he looks across to another side?

No sugar this round. And for pete's sake, keep your damn thumb out of it, will yuh?

Lament with the singer on his wandering peak. The bitter dark music shall outdeep all your prim little dears

Rejoice because I love.

I love everything that has breath above the sun.

I carry poetry on.

Well — it will be a magnificent defeat anyway.

A pompous damn brock, he'd better be lookin the black road and the hard lot of the free

giant form

each word leading its own changing life

WHAT IS THE SIGNIFICANCE OF ART

On The Eve of Science's Last Barren Festival

those other boys at least thought they had a posterity to write for

Doomed rider in a twilight wood.

A man's soul! The only victim is God.

I am all. I am nothing. Shadow into shadow, blood of the sun seeping upward beyond infinity. Fabulous wings longing down

Let us praise or be silent, end without world (anyhow).

Come on, you stupid fool, talk to The Beautiful Lady!

Who's this old bastard, his craw crammed with tobacco —? the stink thick in his whiskers

"You're Helen's *sister?."*

A smart bunch! quite a disguise — Gitouta here, you baldheaded old stenchbomb you!

Softly

flows the river

— Naked she sleeps on its other bank.

I want her. I want to half-kill her. I want to lie a good long time between her smooth warm thighs. I want her to know I'm alive and then some.

24

Hilda-filda-yeah, that's her name. Hilda . . . Emmanuel
. . . or Heloise . . . I once knew a gal called Hellene
Life into Death — Youth asleep under a rotting tree
there goes that front tire again
long-tailed tiger Jesus what a light bill!
Okeydoak, Mr. Turt, first thing in the morning
— Nosir, they'd never get through . . . 'less maybe you
threw tarpulin over the gun mounts: hell I don't have to
tell you what that Mediterranean sun is like
What's that sniffin' round down there ☐

INSCRIPTION FOR A HEADSTONE

He paused uncertainly, then with a quick movement his fingers closed over the door knob. It must be now; now, before the terror should stop him again if he so much as looked down the long length of the dimly lighted hallway with its hostile, secretive doors opening into the rooms of the people who belonged in this house, (people who could not possibly understand why he should be risking so much in entering her room now); he must go on, must open the door, before it should be forever too late.

David, it is time for school. It is such a lovely day out, you must hurry now, David, it is time you were up. And David finds his shoes after a little search and hurries down to breakfast.

And how can he enter her room now; like a thief in the night bent on murder or assault, when after all he was a guest in their house as Mr. Shayer had taken so much trouble to assure him, both in the car coming here and at breakfast when he had first seen Caroline. Yes, he must not think too much on these things for when he did, his mind always strayed back and away, getting all caught and confused with the little black dog trying to get to its feet and in some way being not a dog at all but a shanty beside the river in Alexandria, Mississippi with Steve swearing at the pasty-faced man, or again becoming, (so that it was hard to keep track of any of it), salesmen asking him did he know that the women in New Orleans, and then stopping to urinate beside the road, always looking back over their shoulders; remembering the tankcar out of Seattle and straining even now, where-ever he might be, to hang on: he must not think.

But as he stands beside her door he can feel his fingers slipping, the wind tugging at him, can again feel the cold and the numbness in his back and arms. There in the hall he can feel the swaying car under him, with up ahead, but not taking any part at all, the wrenching drive and moan of the engine, on and on, in its inhuman drive and loneliness, like a crippled death's head, finding the path of a steel pilgrimage under the charted reach of the snow. Slipping; the buildings and trees are whipping by in an avalanche of memory, and the hideous yawn of a tunnel is the mouth and belly of those nights, and never now can he be whole, being still in the tunnel, lost in the churning wheels, slithering through the entrails of it.

His body draws in on itself, (remembering the gravel under the soft snow), and years later in the hall of this stranger's house he is coming to, all twisted out of shape, getting back into himself slowly and timidly, his body like a stranger's coat into which he is struggling, not quite knowing whether when he has walked away he will not have left some part of it that will be needed later. He can not get back from the little shute and declivity of trampled snow beside the roadbed, having failed to take away everything of himself which he had had there.

David, dear, you will be late. Your mother will be waiting and you must go now. I will see you again tomorrow after school. But sweet, you mustn't, you're getting me all mussed, Don't. You'll ruin my dress. Ah, but don't go away; kiss me . . . a long, long, time.

Even now as he felt the door moving inwards under

the press of his shoulder, he couldn't really be sure that he wasn't back there imagining all this, even as it was in the big room down the hall into which Mrs. Shayer had taken him after the shower in the tiled bathroom; for there lying in the huge, rosy bed with its cool sheets, he had stared about at the walls and furniture, ghostlike in the light coming through the curtained windows from the snow outside; being unable then to tell whether this was real or something he had been imagining back there somewhere. He had a feeling of being lost in some nether world in a place somewhere between this warm, carpet house and the nights in the rain back there, a long time ago.

He felt the need of holding on to this as he had held on to the liftrail of the tankcar, grimly, and with all his strength gripped hard to whatever it was that was so surely slipping away, eluding him.

David, who was John Keats? Read him to me. Beauty is . . . but, David, it is so late. It is so very late. And, David, who was John Keats . . . but don't look at me that way . . . .

A door slammed to somewhere, probably one of the servants coming home from a dance or a party. What if they should find him here? He opened the door wide and stepped into the room.

There was no exclamation from the bed, which, when his eyes became adjusted to the bluish light from the snow outside, he could see quite plainly, even make out the little hump in the blankets where she lay sleeping. He felt relieved that she had not been awake, that she had not seen him enter, for even now it was not too late to go back to the big room, slip into his clothes and steal down and out the door, out of this house and into the snowy void of the street, which could not ever frighten him as being here did.

David, I'll meet you tonight on the courthouse square. And the old clock . . .

"What is it? What do you want here? Why aren't you asleep? He turned quickly and as people move in dreams

28

he was conscious of the steps he was making from where he stood (being lost somewhere between), across to the voice which had shown no trace of fear or anger in finding him here, in this room.

"You must go back now and if you are ill, I'll ring for Margie. She's a good one with sick people. Is it your head? Do you have a headache?"

She had risen on her elbows, sitting up and pulling the bedthings fast about her throat, but with no show of fear nor with any suggestion in her manner that there was anything harmful in his presence there in her room so late at night.

"I wanted to talk to you," he said. His voice seemed unequal to the meaning of the words; as though he had drawn it down from a place remote and unfamiliar to him.

"But it is so late. Tell me in the morning." She reached across to the little nighttable and turned on the small lamp, which she probably used for reading, since bright jacketed books and magazines were revealed, strewn about in reckless disorder on the floor beside her bed.

"Please don't. Turn off the light. I just want to talk to you," he said. Something in his voice reached her; she pressed the lamp switch and once more the light in the room was blue, like the non-existence of light in a dream.

David, if you must go away, you will write to me. You can't go away like this. But David did not hurry home, for it was very late. But I won't let you go away. And David looks into the face of the girl he loves. Won't let you go away. David . . . David . . .

He could sense her room, the strangely unreal and frightening feeling of a woman's room, pushing its way into his world, crowding him out as an intruder and thrusting him back, back to the hands and claws.

What's your name? David what? Why'n hell didn't yu say so. Second line over, come on get that lead out. Where duh think yu are anyway? A God-damned picnic or what? Yeah, Shut your trap. David, you will come back?

"What do you want to talk about?" she asked.

When she had said it so simply, and in her friendly, girl-

29

voice, he knew the hopelessness of it. He had nothing to say to her.

The feel of her room was growing more deeply into him. It had a smell the litter of leaves and sticks which, with a long pole, he had snaked out of a muskrat's hole that day in the fall, when he had gone fishing with his father. His father had broken its back with the butt end of his bamboo fishing pole, striking again and again in great anger against it; and after, when it had ceased to struggle and was dead, somehow it was not all there; something of it was gone, not to be found in the mangled heap of fur and blood. And he was sure that his father too, had felt the something gone that his blows had not been able to touch, for he had said nothing during all the long walk home.

But in its nest had been this same sweet and frightening smell which was coming now to him in her room; forcing him away as one who did not belong. The hands and claws were beckoning, and he was become lost, between.

Got a cigarette, kid? Christ a'mighty, that's a good one. Never been west of Chi . . . . . but David come back . . . .

"Talk about? Why I don't know. Tell me . . . do you go to school? Do you have far to walk, getting there, I mean?" he said, standing awkwardly, uncomfortable in the pajamas Mrs. Shayer had found for him in her son's room, which, she said, was never disturbed while he was away at college; he liked to know where to find things, but just this once, and she didn't think he'd find out about it anyway.

"Yes, and it's great fun; some of the jolliest kids ever. Dad drives me in going to the office," then after a pause, "Did you ever have a girl? At home I mean. I'm worried, mother doesn't allow me to go out, says I'm too young. But all the fellows and girls go to dances and around and I don't see why I can't. I'm sixteen. How old are you?"

He knew that it was no good to talk to her, but something that he had wanted was his, merely by staying here near her, and he was afraid to go back, and away, risking the loss of it.

He wondered if she would understand if he were to tell

her about the pasty-faced man or the little dog. What would she say if he were to tell her how he had first seen the little dog, thrown clear of the train wheels, cut squarely in two, the black legs and the stubby little tail rolling over and over down the bank, while the head and fore feet were thrown almost to his feet; tell her how he saw the mouth open and grin up at him the instant before the blood started to stream out of it and down the draggled little chest; tell her how then he saw it try to stand up, the little half dog trying to get up from the ground, with torrents of blood at last covering, and becoming, the little dog, trying to get to its feet.

The pasty-faced man was harder to tell about.

"Yes. I had a girl at home. I was as old as you are, then," he said.

"How long ago was that?" she asked.

"Just a year ago," he said.

"Why did you go away? Was someone unkind to you?" she asked.

"No, not that, my father was out of work and I couldn't stand to be around, in the way like that,"

"Don't you have any brothers or sisters?"

"Yes, too many."

"I don't see how you can say such a thing."

Suppose I don't call you, David? Are there any retreats in the hills or in the temples of the spreading heart? Were you asleep when they took you, David? Do you see with these eyes, hear with these . . . David why do you look at me like that? Circumventing the shoals of the skull . . . . ludicrosities lifting angel hands in praise . . . . David, we never, never coerce the instruments of sleep in the sanctified creating of the night. Let the deft little pinwheels of destruction career over the brink, finding peace, buoyant in the salvage of a suffocated sleep. David the pageant is an echo and a reality . . . .

Suddenly he was crying. He had not thought to cry.

He started for the door and in a moment he felt arms encircling his shoulders. They were warm and very soft.

"Come, get into bed with me."

31

She was leading him as one would lead the blind across a busy street: When he would have drawn away, the insistence of her arms carried him along, drawing him into the warmth and purity of her bed as though he had always belonged there.

And when they were together there in the nest she did not draw away, but with a great and profound wisdom, she thrust her warm, animal body against his.

"You poor little baby, go to sleep. I'll hold you very tightly, oh so tightly, and you must not be afraid, must not be afraid of me, little baby."

Her arms were prayers; around him. The light from the snow was cold and unfriendly. He no longer noticed it but he did not stop crying. In his mind, though, there were no tears; the tears were coming from far back, in the time he had been afraid to cry.

Now, he felt in all his being as his throat had felt in the benediction of warm coffee, down stairs at supper; the coffee like a warm, little animal nosing its way in a delicious warmth through him; seeking a home perhaps, and creating one.

She was becoming less like the thing she was.

"Father promised to phone Mr. Dirks the very first thing in the morning. I'm sure he will be able to use you in his store. You will be allright. Don't be afraid of anything."

He could not for a time realize anything of it: her body strange and choiring in the thunder of its thoughtless vision, was shielding more than there are words to tell of.

"Don't be afraid. Please don't be afraid."

Another feeling unrelated to the compassion she had experienced at the sight of his tears, was rising within her; and it was she who was now bewildered and afraid.

A milk wagon groaned off somewhere down the street.

"Perhaps you had better go back to your bed now," she said.

But he could not go back. He must not go back, must hold on to her, must not let her slip away as everything else had done, becoming words and faces, struggling to life from back there, must go on holding the something in her body that understood and was strong enough to draw up a screen and a veil over it, so that Steve might not be forever saying to the pasty-faced man . . . . .

You bastard, if you so much as touch him, I'll break every bone in your God-damned neck if it's the last thing I ever do . . . . . and the man's face twisted and white looking, trying to upset his head, the chin struggling up over his shoulder, trying to turn his head upside down, and Steve saying that he was just like that through and through: it was not safe to go back to the room across the hall; too much was awaiting him there.

David, the wild flowers were everywhere last summer. and I was so lonely . . . . you were not there. I picked a nice bunch, just for you; but they wilted during the night. David . . . . come back . . . .

"Why did you stare at me so at supper time? I'm sure mother noticed, and father was so disappointed that you didn't answer his questions, after he had been kind enough to take you out of that smelly place and bring you home."

She was frightened now, but she still held him to her, while she listened for some explanation in the beat of her heart and the scraping of the tree boughs at the window; he was for her no longer the little lost boy crying his pain in the night.

"You must go now. It will be daylight soon. You must go now. I don't understand you at all. You must go now," she said.

A faint light was beginning to grow outside the window, reaching long fingers into the gloom of the room. It was as though it was hunting for something, jealous of something within the room that it could not share. The world would soon be awake and what had been done yesterday would be done again as it would be done again on the morrow.

Come back. Only come back.

"Caroline, Caroline," he said. "Caroline, Caroline . . . . "

□

33

I THOUGHT I'D DIE LAUGHING

When she's already to step out again after the slow up
for the tressel Jim an' me hands it over an' up the rail
hopi'n to get inta someplace away from the dicks, an' just
then I sees an empty a couple cars back. I yells at Jim an'
we drops off an' waits till she gets along side an' we piles
in, feelin' that it's some break just divin' in an empty this
way, an empty what's got her door open at that.

Well, we no more'n gets set when I spots this dame sittin'
over all by her lonesome not even takin' much notice of
Jim an' me when we piles in. I sees there's three other guys
in the box an' that they's all got their eye on this dame
sittin' over in the corner all on her own. An' I gets thinkin'
all in a flash as we gets settled down that in a couple hours
it's gonna be darker than hell an' if I don't get next to this
little piece . . . well, I'd see to that al'right.

But this guy Jim I keeps thinkin', maybe he's got some
of his damn fool notions about this now, same as he had in
Dallas when I lets that little punk have it what's been
comin' around. I just lands a nice one, not hard either, an'

the little lady has to crack his crummy head on the flop door-sill. We beats it then and Jim keeps sayin', "Yuh had no right to do that. Did yuh see his face? He's out clean for keeps an' y'u had no right I'm tellin' y'u, hy'u hadn't oughta done it." Well, I don't want any more a that "murderer" stuff from Jim. Yuh can see how it would get to a guy after while. I'm takin' things as they comes but I don't hanker on any more a that kinda talk, specially from a square shooter like Jim is.

So's we're coastin' along see'n corn an' such like out the door . . . Indiana, I guess it was . . . we's comin' up from Louisville goin' to Chi, when I gets an idea I might as well be gettin' acquainted seein' as how things would be after it's gone dark; an' I tells Jim I'm gonna stir around a bit. I mighta knowed he'd start actin' his crazy stuff but I didn't look for him to get so sore as he did. "She's justa kid, lay off. Do you want these guys messin' around her too," he says, an' I can see it's justa sob stunt an' that he's not anxious for me to get hep to the dame either, "Just sit tight'n smear the first guy what makes a move," he says, an' I tells him that's my idea of a laugh. As after I gets mine I ain't given a damn if every guy on the run between here an' the Golden Gate gets his. But Jim's got on his bee bonnet an' won't listen to anything I says. "Just sit tight an' keep your pants on or I'll let y'u have it proper," he says, an' I'm not after any argument with my side-kick, even if he's a little soft in the head sometimes.

About that time one a these guys starts jawin', an' since I figures I'll just have to wait until Jim's asleep or I gets a chance to do a stretch a courtin' after it's dark, whether he's asleep or not, I moves over to where they is, to see what the blokes has to say.

One a these guys has somethin' looks like a spear or one a these sword things like they has in the movies an' the little guy what's sittin next to him pips up askin' this other guy what the hell it is anyway. Well this queer duck with the big knife says, D' you see that old box over there?" We sees it all right. It's an old lemon crate an' its just about a foot from where this dame is sittin'. "Well watch," he says, an' he hauls back an' wham this long knife thing slams square into the middle of one of these lemons what's painted on the box. The dame sorta screams an' I'm not blaming her much since this knife has just missed her arm by inches. Jim comes over an' is all set to mix it up with this bloke when he says, "I beg your pardon but you was perfectly safe. I have never slipped on a throw in ten years."

An' he goes on to tell as how he's an artist with a knife an' makes his bread an' soup peggin' it around to fairs an' carnivals an' such like. Jim tells him to keep the damn thing where it belongs an' I'm thinkin' he's right since I wouldn't want this knife comin' my way after I sees what he done with that little lemon on the box.

"Say, what the hell's the use of stallin'? Let's get together on this dame business. "The guy what says this is a tough lookin' bird lookin' like he belonged in the carnival with this other guy, he's that big an' ugly in his pan, besides which he has a long scar not healed yet what he never got in no Sunday School Picnic either. The dame starts to moan sorta an' Jim tells this gorilla to shut his face or he'll be havin' another scar on it what'll not come off when he washes, if he ever does. An' this guy's so damn dirty you'd think his shirt was walkin' away. Just then the little guy what'd been speakin' to the carn man ups an' says as how we had oughta take a vote or something.

There's no use in goin' through this I'm thinkin' since it's pretty clear anyway, about the dame I mean. An' I'm all set when Jim comes over an' I can see his face is all white like it was the time he plants that guy in New Orleans what's been foolin' aroun with that kid, an' since I'm not after any run in with my pal I tells them to go to hell, I'm votin' hands off the dame. Jim looks that damned pleased that I'm feelin' that maybe it's worth it when this big guy with the scar says as how the votes tied up with me'n Jim on one side an' him an' the little guy votin' for the dame.

I'd always been tellin' Jim as how you could get away

36

with anything if yuh keeps your sense of humour, so before this guy with the knife gets a chance to side in I explains my idea, which is a pip. I tells them to let this guy cut off a piece of her hair with this big-time knife throwin' he's been braggin' so much about an' if he don't make the grade why the dame's anybody's what wants her, an' no more talk or waitin' around.

I figures this guy ain't good enough in a freight what's bumpin' all over the lot an' besides it's gettin' dark damn fast anyway. Well, anything for a laugh an' I thought it'd be some joke on Jim since he wouldn't have no come back after this guy loses the election an' I'd be gettin' next to this shy little dame after all, keepin' my sense of humour besides.

Jim gets as bats as hell sometimes an' this was sure one a the times. He tells us how we must be crazy to even think up such a thing an' starts tellin' us it's inhuman or something like that, when this guy with the scar wants to know what he's so beefed about since Jim's gettin' it square all around, and besides, he says he's got a notion not to wait any more on this fool knife business anyhow.

It's gettin' darker all the time an' I tells Jim if he wants his little American womanhood protected he'd better shut up an' let the guy with the knife do his stuff. So Jim gets these two guys to promise they'll blow the first time she slows down if they lose the election. I'm not trustin' these monkeys much but I figures Jim ain't got a chippies chance in a church anyway; an' just then I'm thinkin' as how what I says to Jim about American womanhood ain't so bad either, nothing like that good ole sense of humour.

Weel, we gets it all fixed. The dame's to stand against the closed box door as the light's comin' in from across that way, what there is of it. The knife fellow's to get three tries an' if he don't clip off some hair the election's lost.

Jim looks kinda sick but he goes over to get the dame figurin' I suppose as how there ain't much else he can do. He's talkin' soft like to her an' I sees as how I won't get on to this guy Jim in a month of Sundays. An' all the while it's gettin' darker outside an' I can just make out a woman putterin' around in one of the fields but it's so dark I can't figure what she's doin' . . . besides it's a rough leg a road an' the ole crate's wobblin' all over the place.

Well, after a time Jim gets the dame set an' the guy with the knife squares off, fast like he's in a hurry to get some place. We all just stand there hardly breathin', least I ain't, but the guy with the scar looks on like he's at a Burlesque or something, his eyes just eatin' up what there is of her. Anyway I just has time to see that there ain't much to her . . . just a young kid like Jim says she is . . . an' that she ain't cryin' now, just standin' there waitin', like she don't care one way or the other, when this knife artist guy lets fly.

She's got some of her hair fluffed out on the side of her head, but if this guy aims to slice off any he's all wrong, since he never touches it. I sees it's just as Jim has put it, an' that big club of a knife still sorta switchin', plumb inta a couple inches a wood, an' her caught up, hanging there twisted over where the knife has landed smack over her right eye . . . pinned to the wood in the door.

The whole thing has come off so fast I sorta gets the notion somehow they'd all been scared stiff an' wantin' to get it over. The knife guy seems to me hasn't even taken aim but just lets go with all the juice in his arm, sorta like he knows all along what's gonna happen but don't care much . . . or maybe after all his hot air about how good he is at throwin' knives, he done it on purpose.

Anyway I tells this yarn to a bloke what I teams with after Jim's gone an' he does a lota talkin' about wishin' he'd been there to see it, an' somethin' as how the knife musta looked like a cross juttin' outa her cheek that way an' that this knife artist guy musta been payin' expiation for all the pain and sin in the world when he lets her have it through the head thata way . . . But hell, I ditched that guy in a hurry . . . I'm not so much up on that kinda talk an' all I know is she did get it pretty an' that I think's it's a damn waste a dames doin' a thing like that whether he's figurin' on it or not.

There ain't much more to tell. The guy with the scar an' the little half pint drops off the next time she slows up an' I'm hopin' it's over a bridge at the time since I don't like these guys much. An' I keeps wonderin' how they feels winnin' the election that way an' the more I thinks about it the more I sees the humorous side of it what with the losin' like that after they'd won, seein' as how this guy never took so much as a hair outa her head.

Jim takes her down; layin' her careful like on some straw he's raked up off the floor. An' all the time he's sayin' there ain't no right for it to happen, over an' like he's in his sleep, talkin' to her as though she ain't deader than a rat, which she is.

An' this champion knife artist don't say a damn thing, just starin' out at the lights an' houses passin', an' after a while he gets up slow and walks out the door, with her tearin' up track some too, goin' down a hill at the time.

All night Jim sits there talkin' to her like she wasn't dead an' I'm feelin' pretty flukey along 'bout mornin', what with him talkin' like a loon to a stiff like that all night, when I looks up an' sees the head of a damn brakeman lookin' down over the side an' in to where we is. That's enough for me an' I tries to get Jim to come along since I'm not figurin' on gettin' mixed up with no bulls on a thing like this, anyway y'u look at it. But Jim just sits there smoothin' out her hair an' talkin' to her like he don't know what's goin' on anymore. Well, I blows figurin' as I do that my neck's as good as the next guys an' I'm not gonna lose it even if Jim's set on losin' his.

I never bumped inta Jim again an' I'm thinkin' as how he mighta got the chair for all I know. But they musta had some time gettin a jury to believe that a guy what ain't got a knife or anythin' coulda made that hole in her head. Course they coulda said he'd throwed it out but still that wouldn't tell how a guy could jam it all the way through like that. Besides them juries is so damned crooked they can't see straight how hard they try.

An' when I tells guys the story they think I'm off my can wantin' to know how any knife artist could work out in a space the width of a box . . . that's all right with me, but what gets me is that they don't see what I alwa's say is the humorous side of the thing.

But any way you look at it most guys ain't got much sense of humour, an' I'm figurin' as how that's what's stoppin' Jim when that brakie pops his dome in at us. It's got me out of a lota tight spots an' I'm damned glad I don't look at things the way guys like Jim do, an' I always say it's the ole sense of humour does it.   □

THE SKATERS

It was very still and lonely now beside the river. If any human had been here this hour he would have remarked the strangeness of this winter's night, would have sensed perhaps the pulsing loneliness of this thing created of night and snow and loneliness.

But he could not have felt the wonder and beauty without wishing to somehow arrest and make fast and secure the part of himself that would feel drawn to the something here.

If you have watched a bird flying away in the dusk over your head on the mission birds have at this evening time you will better understand how anyone in the night beside this river would feel hurt and frightened at being only what he was. He would feel only the sense of his corporal presence and would surely realize it insufficient to the knowledge needed to become a part of this thing of night and loneliness.

He would have been a liver in cities . . . the definite little men who live in little cities built to a giant's plan.

I would not speak of that . . . we are not snakes to crawl from out that which we are into what we cannot ever be.

I am trying to say that the loneliness and desperate

wisdom of the river this winter night would be an act and an achievement not needing the presence of any human to call it into being.

I spoke of the bird because I myself could not visualize the river in its impersonal life tonight and I wished to set up something that you as well as I could understand, hoping in that way to find the courage to go on to the saying of the thing that the river is.

I thought to say it so you would understand but I cannot. What I have to say has little to do with what the river is under its snow and ice tonight. I want to tell you of the death today of someone I love.

After thinking of many ways in which it might be beautifully told I finally decided to tell it in this way. You will understand that I do not feel about it in this way, but I have already told you that the mystery of the river is not to be in anything which I may say to you of it . . . it may be that only one such as myself who has had a direct communication from the river could understand what there are no words to tell of.

I thought of doing it in this way. I would write the history of this river, a history covering one day. Early this morning, I would say, there was a light fall of snow; later in the day a thick blanket of snow fell covering and obscuring all traces of the life which had moved over the ice, and finally, I would go on, toward evening the snow ceased to fall and what there was of everything that had been on the river today was now forever gone, written under in the stillness and the sleep of the snow.

And all the time I am telling you of what I would have said I am telling you my story and the story is all in the words . . . she is dead. and what I am saying I say through fear, a fear that you will not understand that her death would be clear if it were possible to make eternal some part of her which was not lost in death but is secure somewhere in the feeling of the things said to you of the night and the river; not, you will understand, in the feeling I or you might have in the night beside the river where she died, but in the comfort of the unreality I would, by saying these things, make real for myself and for her.

The loneliness I spoke of as being of the river is really mine and I am trying to push it far enough to make it hers too. I cannot, you must see, do this by any method in the telling of it but only by concentration on the few hints I have received by thinking of the river and the bird as somehow a message from her.

And in the desire to tell this, without losing that sense of kinship with the loneliness of the river and the bird flying into the dusk, I thought of making the footprints in that early morning snow the record of a pilgrimage into the haven of this loneliness.

But always I was brought up, leaning on the fabric of the idea, not being able to quite forget the tragic concreteness in the number of footprints coming down to the river's edge and the number of footprints which were made in leaving. That was to have been the history covering one day, of the river in the snow . . . she had brown hair . . . and I was afraid that in the record of this day I could not, however hard I tried, forget that the footprints had ever been anything other than the symbols which I had made of them.

Now in despair of ever telling this thing as it is to me I would go to the river tonight and live for myself the story which I cannot tell . . . but I am afraid . . . perhaps this is all empty and untrue! The strange thoughts which I have tried to make clear to you regarding how I feel with her dead are less strange surely than the careless gift of the river in taking her in death, to be . . . for those who are alive tonight . . . with the dead. And that is what I cannot understand. I can understand the reality of the footprints in the snow but . . .

I cannot tell you what it is that I am trying to say, I want only to tell that she is dead and that it is not possible for me to know this in the way I can feel the inhuman beauty of this river which has killed her. It as though I am become heir to the reasoning of the river and the bird . . . and I cannot hope to tell you of it.

In the morning there were footprints leading down . . . but this is not the history of a river, covering one day . . .

But I want only to tell you that she is dead and   ☐

THE PLAIN OF COOLDREVIN:

The Story of a Mother Disillusioned by Her Sons

Mrs. Grady wasn't thinking of the strike as she walked along the street fronting the railroad; it was Friday afternoon and the boys would be wanting their haddock at five o'clock. She strode briskly into Samerton's "Fresh Meat and Vegetable Mart," her big hands busy at the clasp of her cloth purse. Three pounds at fourteen cents: three fours are twelve, and carry one; three ones are three and one is four-forty-two cents — yes, that was right. And with the bread and cheese, the half pound of tub-butter, the day's shopping came to a dollar and — wait: she had nearly forgotten Tom's smoking tobacco — fourteen and two pennies tax, sixteen, and a dollar three cents; $1.19. Within her budget.

She walked around to the back door. In all her twenty-odd years in the house, she had never entered it by the front door, not even on Sunday; that was a special privilege reserved for the boys. Flinging her shawl, a present from Eddie, on its nail in the cellar-way, she tore open the package containing the fish; began the preparation for supper. She hummed as she worked: *Ah, sure 'twas the truth in her eyes. tum tum, that made me love Mary, that made me te ta tum tum.*

Big Tim's favorite song. Bless his old heart, dead these many years. She sobbed quietly, in a private, almost lighthearted way. Tim, her husband, had been killed when the steam crane in which he worked upset, spilling the scalding water from its tank over him. The accident had occurred five years before, and for as many years at the same time in the afternoon, Mrs. Grady remembered his song and cried for his dear memory.

Ah, he'd been a rough one, he had; beatin' her soundly every Saturday night — and his big voice soft and endearing later: "Sure, Molly, my pet, and I'm not the mon to be wishin' ye ill." And he wasn't. But in his cups — the big braw of a bluffer . . .

Sure 'twas the truth ta tum dum . . . The slam of the front door screen: Eddie. She swabbed her face with a dishtowel; it wouldn't do at all to have Eddie catch her "at it" again. He'd given her a taste of his old man's temper the last time it had happened. "Let the old one count the worms in peace," he had said. Count the worms, indeed. But here he was, his huge fist on her shoulder.

"How's it comin', lady? Smells good."

Her boys all called her "lady"; that is, all but Davey. Davey called her "mother." Davey her youngest, her wee boy, her little light . . .

"Quit starin' and get some meat behind it; let's get it on the table before the world ends. I've got to get off to see Nora."

She gave the frying-pan a jerk, liberating the fish from the stuck fat at the bottom.

"Sure and what's keepin' Tom? Hope he ain't mixin' hisself up with those doin's over to the mill. Gettin' his head battered, he will."

"Oh, fuss away, He's prob'bly over to Tony's Pool Room. Fat lot he cares to mix up in the mill thing." Eddie peeled off his coat and sat down at the table; his thick fingers made two of a piece of her homemade bread.

Soon Tom came in, his face sour under her questioning look; he fell to without preamble. They ate the fish and cheese in silence. Over coffee, Eddie asked her if she had had any word from Davey. Ah, Davey; her wee one, her —

"Not in betterin' a month. The dear heart's likely too busy with his studyin' duties." The boys grunted. This was Davey's second year in an Eastern college.

"The dear heart! You're bloody free with your words, lady. Dear heart! The little mush is prob'bly wastin' his time in great shape now's he has an education to show him how to do it better," Tom said. Eddie didn't laugh, but she could see that he approved.

It was after the table had been cleared and the boys had gone that the special delivery letter came. "Sign here." "Ah, sure an' I will, to be sure," and all the while her eyes big with the knowledge that the letter concerned her Davey. The postmark: sure it was — but the handwriting, that queer slant and the letters dark and heavy on the paper — this was not Davey's writing. Mrs. Grady ripped the envelope across, tearing off a strip of letter; she could never get it to tear just along the edge. My dear Mrs. Grady:

This is to inform you that your son David was drowned last night in the Hudson River near . . .

The letters wriggled like snakes, a very shindig of snakes. Her big face wrinkled, the eyes closing slightly. She fainted, upsetting the kitchen table as she fell.

Eddie didn't get home until eleven (Tom often stayed out until the early morning).

"But, lady, it's too late tonight. Wait till daylight. I'll send the wire then. It can wait," Wait! sure it could wait, and her boy, her little light . . .

"Shivers take ye! I'll be doin' it meself. A fine lot of loafers. Drunks! No good drunks. And how you made his life a torture. You an' your old man. Naggin' him, houndin' him. 'Cause he weren't like ye. For he had it in his head to be likin' that poetry stuff. Why didn't he get a job? Why didn't he do this, do that? Not lettin' him any peace . . . and now he's . . ."

"Lady, for Pete's sake let up. He'll keep till mornin'.

An' they'll send him home, be sure of that. They al'a do."

That night was Davey's. She soothed and comforted him; told him not to mind the shenanigans of the boys. Drat thim. Neither worth a halfmeasure of barley. Dashin' round like two dogs after the girls and the drink. Not even holding steady jobs. "The mill's too hot; and what's it get you: look at the old one — done to a turn with the bones boiled out of his hide. Not for me, no siree." Oh, Davey, 'twas lucky to be carryin' insurance on Tim. That was your chance. Your turn on the poetry. But sure, if you hadn't gone out there, if you hadn't left your mother's side, you'd be al . . .

She could remember the way he used to sit in that old plush chair in the parlor — he was such a wee thing then — reading, his little face still with the wonder of the book:

Alas for the voyage, O High King of Heaven,
Enjoined upon me,
For that I on the red plain of bloody Cooldrevin
Was present to see.

Davey, what have they done to ye? Why have they wanted to take ye from your lady's side?

With the first staining of dawn on the paper flowers of her room, the first distant crowing of a cock, she fell asleep.

"Tom, in the name of Patrick stop blubberin'. Serves you right. They should 'a' knocked the lights out of you for what's the thing you've done. You had it comin'. Try to take it like somethin' like a man."

More trouble, always something to worry her with the boys. Then Mrs. Grady remembered. Davey! Ye couldn't, God; not to me. Tom was hunched over the table when she entered the kitchen. She could make out the beaten emptiness of his face; the eyes dark and swollen in the confusion of bruises and bloody cuts. She felt no pity; nothing. What ever had happened, and Eddie was right, " 'e had it comin' to 'im." But she could not refrain from asking for news of what had happened to Tom.

Eddie, his voice without emotion, told her. Tom had

been waylaid and beaten by mill strikers; he had been serving as a company deputy, turning in the names of those who took part in the picketing. A company-scab. Merciful Heaven! If Big Tim, from where he was now, could only see his eldest son — a stool pigeon.

> *I set my face*
> *To the road here before me,*
> *To the work that I see*
> *To the death that I shall meet.*

Ah, the stern beautiful words. and Davey's boyish voice growing deep with their wonder. Tom left the room; the dirty, smoke-streaked light of the morning like a cross on his bent back. Eddie remained, a mug of cold coffee fast in his great hand. Mrs. Grady put on her shawl, Her boys wouldn't do so much as send a telegram which would bring home the dead remains of their brother — no, *her son*, not their brother, not thim; her own darling wee light. She adjusted her skirt; pushed back a last stubborn strand of white hair.

The door-bell! Likely the Father. Ah, the dear man — so quick to come to comfort his flock. She straightened a rug as she passed through the living-room. Eddie sat, stolid, a pipe between his teeth, waiting to hear the Father's first words.

"Mother." By the Saints! Davey! Eddie jerked to his feet and made for the front of the house. Above their mother's fallen body, the two brothers stared at each other.

"You dirty whelp. Now what's the bloody likes of this? Scarin' the lady near to her death." Eddie bent and lifted the old woman's body, carried it over to the overstuffed couch, put it tenderly down.

"It was part of an initiation; the fellows of my fraternity thought of it. Of course, I didn't like it, but there was nothing I could do — and besides, Mother had only one night of thinking it."

One night, Davey.

For that I on the red plain of Cooldrevin . . .

48

Eddie would have called the doctor to attend his mother had he not just then remembered a promise to meet Nora at nine o'clock; her mother was going to attend Stations of the Cross and they would have the house to themselves. Davey brought her to with a dipper of cold water.

Suppers on Saturday night had ever been dull for Mrs. Grady; her boys were always too anxious to be done and off on their dates, to have any time for talk with her. This one was different. The whole world was dying in her heart as she listened to Davey telling the boys of his fraternity, and of his new brothers. "Frat." Now what did that mean? And this initiation thing — if to be hurt entitled you to membership, then what could *she* not join, O High King of her little Davey's Heaven? □

BUT THERE WAS STILL
ANOTHER PELICAN IN THE BREADBOX

Once you were the only lady harpoonist on the Great Banks
Could whistle the Serbian Anthem while standing with one foot
Tied behind your head and the other behind the Captain's
Now you attend ceramics class on alternate Tuesdays
And hope to put a music-box pet comfort pan
On the market; for your interest in the underdog
Has, in these gentle surroundings, extended itself
Even unto his petty rival, the cat.

*Patchen (left) with Anais Nin and Hugh Guylor
at a party on Bleecker Street, New York City, 1940.*

*Patchen and Miriam in Rhinebeck, New York, 1935,
where he wrote "Before the Brave".*

In lonely houses — at least, an apple; songmaker, stranger... carnivorous lamb — violent
night hairy night — easy damns it O
Life the Giver
all under the falling calling
for peace
grace
and Mercy
O let the kind lead the kind
Sorrow, my meek hearts, only sorrow and not
Sit down and make yourself to hell. From this
day, all sickness and poverty and fear are abolished
Hatred will keep a little longer. O and when the
Who *is* that on the balcony?
"An immense din of drums, horns, flageolets,
gongs, both small and inferior, mingled with the
yells of a really frantic crowd, drown the shrieks
of the sufferers, upon whom the earth is shoveled and
stamped down by thousands of cruel fanatics, who
dance and jump upon the loose mould so as to force
it into a compact mass through which the victims
of this interesting sacrifice cannot grope their way!
HERE LIES J. FREBERSHAM DORK · LATE OF (I had
me reasons for leavin Seamis City, you bet...) 5 six
soaking wet, dark blond hair, In gaol We Trust
tatooed on his aine behind, wouldn't ye ken now

Manuscript sample from "The Story of Jeremiah Dork
and the Kiladian Forest", published in this volume.

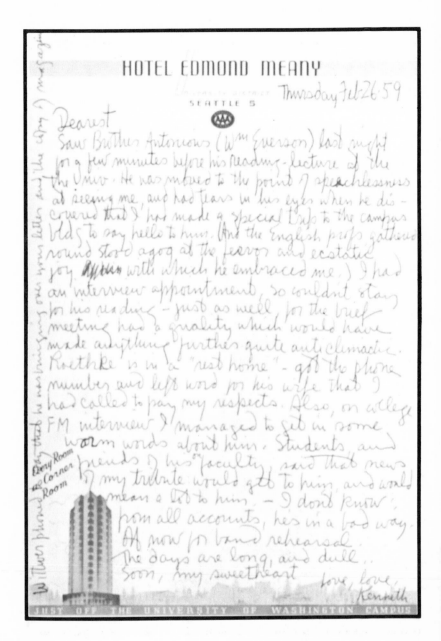

HOTEL EDMOND MEANY

SEATTLE 5

Thursday Feb 26·59

Dearest

Saw Brother Antonious (Wm Everson) last night for a few minutes before his reading-lecture at the the Univ. He was moved to the point of speechlessness at seeing me, and had tears in his eyes when he dis-covered that I had made a special trip to the campus bldg to say hello to him. (And the English profs gathered round stood agog at the fervor and ecstatic joy with which he embraced me.) I had an interview appointment, so couldn't stay for his reading — just as well, for the brief meeting had a quality which would have made anything further quite anti-climactic. Roethke is in a "rest home" — got the phone number and left word for his wife that I had called to pay my respects. Also, on college FM interview I managed to get in some warm words about him. Students, and friends of his faculty, said that news of my tribute would get to him, and would mean a lot to him. — I don't know; from all accounts, he's in a bad way. Off now for band rehearsal. The days are long, and dull.. Soon, my sweetheart

love, love,
Kenneth

Letter and envelope from Patchen to Miriam, 1959.

AIR MAIL

Mrs Kenneth Patchen
2340 Sierra Court
Palo Alto, California

Examples of Patchen's numerous paintings.

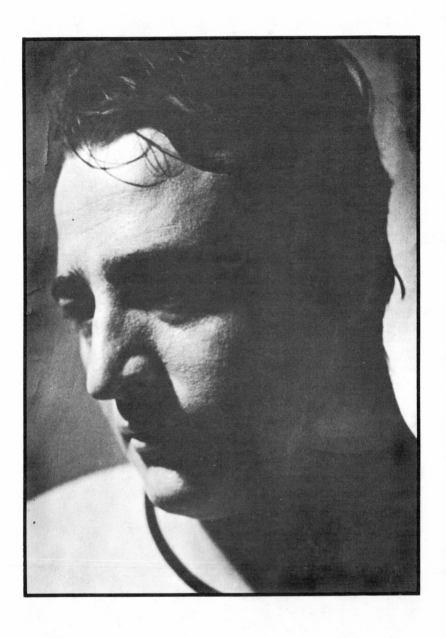

TO A BEAST OF THE SLUMS

Ah, house-ephant, who has tethered you here?
The most heartless oaf would not leave
A pig to root about in such filth;
be a loveable sort.

This tolerant clairvoyant, who lets
Your hulk to downy chicks and molting crows;
To pluffing stoat nervy tossalot —
What murder only guesses money already knows.

Damn! you are an ugly brute!
Your snout reddened on this drab lettuce —
Precisely the kind of devil's boot
This walking hell was bound to get us.

WHILE THE GREEN TREES THEY GREW

Everyone has heard the ever-recurring tale
Of the lady'sman coachman and his grand dream
Of having one day his own broad estates
With a bright red pumphouse in a cluster
Of haystacks right by the maids' dorms
And a pal or two to get bottled up
For a free and easy read starting and ending with
'My Life Is Like The Great Speckled Bird
That Smells The Twiney Worm A-eatin' Of The Perkiest Lord'
And maybe Dolly Laundeveere to be shying in
Her hair all soft and dark
As the inside of a little cub's fist
And wouldn't her stovepipe-lidded old man just squint up
At the only weathervane in this county
Ever had twenty proposals of marriage
Before they could court-order it into that red silk bathingsuit
'For O my life . . . my life, boys, it is like . . .'

While the green trees they grew
And the wind . . . why, hell, what else could it do? . . . it blew
And The Great Speckled Bird went flashing by
With a flaming of its mane and a roaring of its one great
        and angry eye

60

"WELL, HERE I AM"

Well, here I am . . still just a wide-eyed countryboy.
Assumed that there . . up there . . to be conquered by these
madmen with their new surgical instruments: *that* animal
up there watching down! My God!

Well, they've begun to hack away at it. A fleck of
blood on its foot . . . another drop may drown us off . . Up
there that won't matter; step on the flea, and forget it.

Well, so?

So.

OLD WOMEN DISCUSSING THE BIRTH OF A PRINCE

"Ah, and still might he be led,
Half round where the trees walk,
And the green waits in her glossy shed."
"Oh, more would it love him then,
As fat winds upon the fatter waters lean —"
"But look! dear Missy Moon plucks down another hen!"
"And yet . . . ah, yet was he ever more neglected less!"
And they drew their smoldering noses down
Across the stubble of his neck and little chest.

WHO INDEED

What! would you surprise me here at home amongst these baubles,
reminders, remissions, the spent-chest filaments of straddling
coquetries on whose juvenilescence now only grim-visaged sea-
birds string their wash? Ah, great Shakes, yet does this
immoderant pattern disclose still the peppermint-striped music
that swaddled him of Ithaca the rosy scribe, and lower quite
away, but last, that hoary thewed rump in an ill-fitting
bathinggarment to gaze in envy at some yet taller Pythagoras
— and never to know exactly what is meant or what it may be
huff-puffed to symbolize . . . O wordy whiskerers peeping in
under my tentflap, whose borrowed eyes, whose borrowed yap?

Who obliniating th' unmistrusted debauchery
Of medullated falsehood,
Prey of supplebottomed democrites,
Distinguished less than venomously paralleled,
Will'nt himself accentuate —
If thereby accruing thrice?
A'yes, to mistrust such creeds,
Th' languor of trenchant gratuities plunged
Barefoot in mobtubs!
A pity, sirs & dears.
Yet no opprobium, untenability's heir,
May frightfully attach itself to th' still marge,
Or — particularly — to th' juicy centercut.
Nah! nor any taint of illbred compassion
Stain th' greenbacked skirts of your grammar.

THE CHRIST OF THE ANDES

Oh mute figure of stone!
Standing silently through the age
Nations pause and peace is sown,
Yes peace the saga of the sages,
In you is vested a mighty race
Night reveals deep lines in your
     stone face.
May the sun shine on the fated
     day,
When Peace shall stride through
     the world,
And War die and its banner de-
     cay,
Leaving Goodwill's standard un-
     furled
Then thank God on bended knees
No need for the Christ of the
     Andes!

PLEA OF THE INSANE

Oh the strangely, sneering face of
    the moon,
With pity and scorn mingled,
    watches me
It knows that I with this life am
not in tune.
A brooding fear haunts me.
And that moon for others so rare,
Causes me trembling, to sit and
    stare.
It leaves me not in the morn,
But always its spell is on me.
As before my mind, with fear torn,
All reason gone from me,
I see water flow upon a plain
Surely my brain has snapped in
    strain.
And now I am in a dreadful place,
In such a place have they sent me
'Round me each has a soul-strick-
    en face
God with sweet death doth free
    me!
For yet looming in my deadened
    sight,
I see that cursed moon every night.

HAVE MERCY

On a fiery desert thrown,
A young Arab lay dying
Drifted sand by wind blown,
Choked him, brokenly crying
"Water, do I cry in vain?"
Despairing, yet cried again

From The parched sands, a spring,
Burst with gurgling sound.
The buzzards on still wing,
A course westward wound.
As the boy with tearful eyes,
Knelt under the chalky skies.

ASPIRATION

Beauty!
Stark, pulsing, naked beauty,
Unwordly, leering beauty,
Just beyond reach
It mocks man.
At the shrine
Of the unattainable
Man entreats
But for a taste, a sip,
And he would be content,
Having known beauty,
To live with ugliness,
As his companion
At times. Poets, reaching high,
See as in a divine dream;
But from that day forth
Are doomed
To hunger in vain,
Walking the earth
With bewildered, blank faces.

IMPROBABLE REALITIES

When the sea in helpless agony
     whips its shores,
And the battered rocks mouth in
     stricken pain,
A great white swan with angry
     flashing eyes
Brushes away the tattered gar-
     ments of the weary wind
And with motionless wings flies to
     where
A sobbing thing pitches in a steel
     trap,
Watched over by the soul of a
     drunken fat man,
Who, dying of thirst, drinks wine
     from an empty monkey skull
Only to see it run out of a vent in
     his throat.
The Thing is Justice
Under a barbed wire crown,
And through bleeding lips it forms
     the words
"Forgive them, for they know what
     they do."
As the swan falls with broken
     heart,
And the rocks jab the sea into a
     froth of dashing blood
The great god Swine rears back
     his ugly head and sneering -
     ly laughs
As the echoes, pelt the watching
     mountain

TO ALAN SEEGAR

The promise of a golden voice is
    dead
The lute with broken strings will
    sound no more
Your prelude hungered for a full-
    er score
As untried symphonies raced
    through your head.
Alas, that mute the unheard notes
    have fled,
To join with Shelley's in a princely
    store
To soothe The Ruler of that other
    Shore,
Who gleans the harvest of gems
    unsaid
Oh Keeper of that realm where
    poets sing
The songs that death snatched from
    the human race,
Send down a strain from your do-
    main of blue,
So that the soul of man may take
    swift wing
And not be held to earth by time
    or space.
Gladly would I then meet my ren-
    dezvous!

PERMANENCE

If I should say (in jest): Do you recall
The day we spent in quest of woodland
    flowers?
And how a fragrant silence seemed to fall
As safe we stood, unstained by fleeting
    hours?
And you were glad and said the jewel-like
    trace
Of gold in ferns was like a wordless
    prayer;
And drenched and warm with light, I saw
    your face:
All love and wonderment held captive
    there.

There is no bitterness that one may save
Against the film of change and mold of
    tide.
Oblivious, the stars — in dying — wave
A threat of dust; and graves are deep
    and wide.
For time and death are twins, of this be
    sure;
And only dreams and things unsaid
    endure.

REVERSING THE INQUEST

As the hours passed the foreman's boots grew
    larger and more monstrous.
From where he stood in the ditch, up to his knees
    in mud,
He could have reached out his hand and touched them.
The clatter of pick and shovel and the gutteral
    voices of the laborers,
Reached him but thinly, filtering slowly through the
    heavy folds of his leaden brain.
The glittering hugeness of the shoe was blotting
    out the sky;
His children's faces, smiling momentarily, grew
    shapeless and sodden red beneath its enormous sole,
His garden with its shy, friendly little
    flowers was being trampled into the alien
    soil;
Trees were bending, the earth trembled —
    (The weight on his chest was crushing him
    into the cold and mud of the ditch.)
With all his failing strength he flung the pick.
"Well, I'll be damned. That lousy wop musta had
    a touch of sun. He got Bill, did ya say?"

LENIN

Choir, sweet voices of a thundering dawn.
(Hills are reddening on the fringe of desolation.)
Lips, dumb with prophecy, are moving,
    moving to the sternness of a dream;
Waving plumes of sound are advancing
    on the glory of his voice;
In the ashes of his tomb the sturdy feet of a nation
    are stirring in their shackles.
From the nostrils of his faith is blowing the fire
    that shall melt the chains of man.

WHITMAN, 'OUR ALL-AROUNDEST POET,'
IS CULLED BY MARK VAN DOREN

Review of *The Portable Walt Whitman*. Selected, with notes, by Mark Van Doren

There is the oft-told tale, beloved of people who write books about people who write books, that Walt(er) Whitman, accoucheur of Democracy and Applied Phrenology (pronounced bumps), 220 lbs. avoirdupois, white-bearded booted in magnificent black morocco, carrying a stegis in the golden sash-band of his baggy pants, once, finding no razor blades in the next-to-the-top drawer of his mother's chiffonier, where he always kept them, walked 17 miles through a downpour of cats and dogs to return an old battered biscuit tin to a Mrs. Swangleam, also old and battered. The cats and dogs were never explained; nor Whitman either, for that matter.

Though James Q. Miffle did advance the curious theory that W.W. was a human being — and therefore pretty tough going for most people.

We have, then, eight points to consider: one) Did Whitman ever live with a woman in New Orleans? If so,

73

did he like it? Did she like it? two) Where did *Leaves of Grass* come from? From Herman Melville's beautiful poem-in-prose called *Mardi?* (Read it some time.) From *The Countess of Rudolstadt* by George Sand? From Emerson? From Martin Farquhar Tupper? three) Was Whitman a homosexual? Probably. four) Is he a good poet? Yes. five) Great poet? No. But the all-aroundest we've had. six) Was he on the level with his "amativeness," "alimentiveness," "adhesiveness," etc.? Not all together. Who could be? seven) What is his importance? He broke with an out-worn tradition — though now his own voice or "tone" is more stagnating to young talent than any which proceded him. To break with tradition (even a bad job) is good in itself. Anywhere but into the old molds. Experiment is nine-tenths of art; always the *new* — let it be bad; often more interesting, anyway. A bad *new* poem (with heartache and guts) is better than 10 W. Hugh Audens any day in the week. Tell me the point of saying nothing in 629 antique French verse forms. Try chess. Or tiddly-winks. eight) What of Whitman's followers? Well, *you* have Sandburg — N. Corwin, a something in radio — and a Somebody Davenport — etc., etc. The point here is not their lack of dignity (why mention talent?), but just what did old Walt hand them that smells so bad? This cozy, cozy blah-blah about how a lot of funny-named rivers run up and then run down and the sky is oh so *very* blue and the harness-rubbers and the sturdy Sturdy STURDY workmen. All pretty blue too.

In the Civil War days

I see that I need another point nine) to say something about Mark Van Doren's editing job. It's all right. The introduction's all right — level, quiet, competent, dull. The *Leaves* is in. *Democratic Vistas*, in. He could have lopped off about half of the poem called *Specimen Days* without hurting anything.

Whitman, I think, wrote at his highest in these lines — after the Civil War:

74

Lo! Victress on the peaks!
Where thou, with mighty brow, regarding
 the world,
(The world, O Libertad, that vainly con-
 spired against thee;)
Out of its countless beleaguering toils, after
 thwarting them all;
Dominant, with the dazzling sun around
 thee,
Flauntest now unharm'd, in immortal
 soundness
And bloom — lo! in these hours supreme,
 poem proud, I, chanting, bring to thee —
Or mastery's rapturous verse;
 book, containing night's darkness,
And blood-dripping wounds,
And psalms of the dead.

(This poem does not appear in the present selection.)

Before, I said that Whitman was not a great poet. Listen to one:

THE MIDDLE OF LIFE

With yellow pears the land,
And full of wild roses,
Hangs down into the lake.
O graceful swans,
And drunk with kisses,
You dip your heads
Into the hallowed-sober water.

Alas, where shall I find when
Winter comes, flowers, and where
Sunshine,
And the shadows of earth?
The walls stand
Speechless and cold, in the wind
Weathercocks clatter.
    — Friedrich Holderlin
     (1770-1843)

75

And now, after two beautiful poems, a few words from that other, little-known, and logically, greater Walt Whitman:

"Nature (the only complete, actual poem), existing calmly in the divine scheme, containing all, content, careless of the criticisms of a day, or these endless and wordy chatters, And lo! to the consciousness of the soul, the permanent identity, the thought, the something, before which the magnitude even of democracy, art, literature, etc., dwindles, becomes partial, measurable-something that fully satisfies (which those do not). That something is the All, and the idea of All, with the accompanying idea of eternity and of itself, the soul, buoyant, indestructible, sailing space forever, visiting every region, as a ship the sea. And again lo! the pulsations in all matter, all spirit, throbbing forever — the eternal beats, eternal systole and diastole of life in things — wherefrom I feel and know that death is not the ending, as was thought, but rather the real beginning — and that nothing is or can be lost, nor ever die, nor soul, nor matter."

"In the future of these States must arise poets immenser far and make GREAT POEMS OF DEATH. The poems of life are great, but there must be the poems of the purports of life, not only in itself, but beyond itself."

I would defend Whitman against them any day, but I've never felt really warm about him. Burroughs once reported that "his hands were soft and hairy." Maybe that's it — the well-laundered 'tough,' sort of thing. I mean . . . getting into the poems. It's certainly none of my business what he wore or didn't wear. A sad one — every time he really got a whiff of it. Like Melville. Like any other artist in this country who isn't willing to paint his behind with a dollar sign and wave it around in the approved fashion.

To The Sharks

Hart Crane, Whitman's only great follower, jumped off a boat to the sharks.

76

The Poems of Death — the crueler sharks on the land . . .
But let our Walt Whitman, "SALUTE THE WORLD":

> *You olive-grower tending your fruit on*
> *fields of Nazareth, Damascus, or Lake*
> *Tiberias!*
> *You Thibet trader on the wide inland, or*
> *bargaining in the shops of Lhassa!*
> *You Japanese man or woman! you liver in*
> *Madagascar, Ceylon, Sumatra, Borneo!*
> *All you continentals of Asia, Africa, Eu-*
> *rope, Australia, indifferent of place!*
> *All you on the numberless islands of the*
> *archipelagoes of the sea!*
> *And you of centuries hence, when you*
> *listen to me!*
> *And you, each and everywhere, whom I*
> *specify not, but include just the same!*
> *Health to you! Good will to you all — from*
> *me and America sent.*
> *Each of us inevitable;*
> *Each of us limitless — each of us with his*
> *or her right upon the earth;*
> *Each of us allow'd the eternal purport of*
> *the earth!*
> *Each of us here as divinely as any is here.* □

BLAKE

It would be interesting to write of Blake's recent work —
that of the past hundred-odd years, for instance.
In the arms of God and the veil pushed aside.
For William Blake was beautifuled less by life than an
enormous wakening when his body that was shadow merged
with sun and *The Mundane Shell* of poems drawings books
'the angel taught me to do' was shattered

> "Died" 1828 — death-year (Jean-Paul Richter's,
> Beethoven's, too)
> 'he composed and uttered songs to his Maker'
> — "My beloved, they are not mine — no — they
> are not mine." — shattered
> into an Always Always light.
> AH THESE GOLDEN BIRDS ARE ALIVE
> the ecstasy — the Fire the dread and
> Granting Fire — not to know more
> but to be and to feel ALL!

Blake believed.

Kill most people just to think about that.

Not a poem — (Great lyric gift, don't you think?) — but an eye looking through the Infinite.

Not a picture — (Judged at least by the standards of the Artappreciation-course at Dartmouth, say . . .) — but real HONEST TO GOD Beings eternal Beings shaking the dust of the drugclerk's 'mystism' off their bleeding feet.

Honest to God, Blake was.

My dear Friend

Lest you should not have heard of the Death of Mr. Blake I have written this to inform you — He died on Sunday Night at 6 O'clock in a most glorious manner. He said He was going to that Country he had all His life wished to see & expressed himself Happy hoping for Salvation through Jesus Christ — Just before He died His Countenance became fair — His eyes Brightened and He burst out in Singing of the things he Saw in Heaven. In Truth He died like a Saint as a person who was standing by Him Observed. He is to be Buried on Friday at 12 in the morning. Should you like to go to the Funeral — If you should, there will be room in the Coach.

Yrs. G. Richmond

And honest to Blake, God was. William Blake believed this. His new work must be very beautiful.

The Prophetic Books (the earlier, so called Lambeth: VISIONS OF THE DAUGHTERS OF ALBION; AMERICA, A PROPHECY; EUROPE; THE BOOK OF URIZEN; THE SONG OF LOS; THE BOOK OF AHANIA . . . and the two last, and greatest: MILTON and JERUSALEM) are all concerned with man's inadequacy before his true creature who is God; but they also record a vigorous protest against

79

the betrayal of justice and honor and reason by man's misgovernors, against every repression and denial of human freedom — out of no rhetorical vacuum did Blake's spirit greet with blazing eloquence the revolutions in France and America: Blake was perhaps the greatest social realist of his age — the bitter immediacy of his symbolism is as much grounded in the Industrial Revolution in England as it is in his own special 'Country' (of the naked and majestic Soul).

> Shall not the King call for Famine from the heath,
> Nor the Priest for Pestilence from the fen,
> To restrain, to dismay, to thin
> The inhabitants of mountain and plain,
> In the day of full-feeding prosperity
> And the nights of delicious songs?
> Shall not the Councellor throw his curb
> Of poverty on the laborious,
> To fix the price of labour,
> To invent allegoric riches?
> And the privy admonishers of men
> Call for fires in the City,
> For heaps of smoking ruins
> In the night of prosperity & wantonness?
> To turn man from his path,
> To restrain the child from the womb,
> To cut off the bread from the city,
> That the remnant may learn to obey,
> That the pride of the heart may fail,
> That the lust of the eyes may be quench'd,
> That the delicate ear in its infancy
> May be dull'd, and the nostrils clos'd up,
> To teach mortal worms the path
> That leads from the gates of the Grave.

Many have attempted to penetrate the identities of the 'things' in Blake's poems — Geoffrey Keynes, S. Foster Damon, Ellis, Yeats, Sloss, Wallis, etc., etc.: this identification (which I think is the most interesting) is Mr. Damon,

80

and appears in his book, *William Blake, His Philosophy And Symbols*, 1924, O.P.: *Los* (sol) equals What the Poet can know; *Urizen* equals Reason; *Enitharmon* equals Inspiration; *Orc* e. a union of Imagination & Reason; *Tharmas* e. The Senses (of this world); *Luvah* e. The Emotions (from the moon); *Eden* e. The Site of Inspiration; *The Fall* e. Our Entry into the Flesh (and is division); *Elohim* e. Man's Judge; *Shaddai* e. The Accuser; *Lucifer* e. Pride of Self; *Molech* e. The Slayer; *Pahad* e. The Horror at What Has Been Done; *Jehovah* e. The One Who Sees Evil; *Jesus* equals The One Who Sees Good, etc., etc.

   — at an exhibition — 1823 —

> 'While so many moments better worthy to remember are fled, the caprice of memory presents me with the image of Blake looking up at Wainewright's picture; Blake in his plain black suit and rather broad-brimmed, but not quakerish hat, standing so quietly among all the dressed-up, rustling, swelling people, and myself thinking "How little you know who is among you!"'

Blake's bread-and-butter trade from childhood was copper engraving.

> (1779 — to illustrations by others — *A New System of Geography* — *Fencing Familiarized & The Protestant's Family Bible & The Speaker & & & & & & through 1829 more than 50 such jobs

and he illustrated a lot of books too

> (from *Sepulchral Monuments in Great Britian* — 1786 — through *A Treatise on Jodiacal Physiognomy* — 1828 —

17 'illustrations' in all
including

ILLUSTRATIONS OF THE BOOK OF JOB
(*) the greatest achievement in line-engraving since Durer
— the purest of all Blake's recordings with a graving tool: song of the Morning Stars — engraved straight on the copper, without use of acid at all

Blake dreamed of 'the beautiful book' — written, decorated, engraved, printed and illuminated by one creator. He discovered a fluid with which *he simply wrote on the copper plate what he wanted to print* — and this secret died with him.

Blake painted *The Last Judgement* — one of man's noblest expressions. And in 1820, aged 63, Blake did seventeen woodcuts for PASTORALS OF VIRGIL (Dr. Thornton's) — publisher Thornton upon receiving them said: "This fellow must do no more!"

Dr. Thornton, in his preface: 'The Illustrator of Young's *Night Thoughts* and Blair's *Grave*, who designed and engraved them himself. This is mentioned as they display less art than genius, and are much admired by some eminent painters.'
Genius for what, then, Dr. T!
Blake said

IDEAS CANNOT BE GIVEN BUT IN THEIR MINUTELY APPROPRIATE WORDS, NOR CAN A DESIGN BE MADE WITHOUT ITS MINUTELY APPROPRIATE EXECUTION.

Blake spent the last two years of his life making designs for Dante's *Inferno*.
He made a series of Imaginary Heads (at the suggestion of J. Varley — *Man Who Built the Pyramids* — *Ghost of a*

Flea — just pleasant fun for Blake.

Many of the preliminary drawings for his engravings have been lost.

Forty years after his death he was (to all 'practical' purposes) forgotten. Swinburne and Rossetti excited themselves for him.

The first show of his work was in 1876; the second in 1906.

Blake's drawings are like Blake's poems — which is more than can be said for the drawings of any other human.

When someone asked the Angel whether it liked Blake's drawings, it said (and very seriously): If you are fully capable of Purity and have the Wisdom of Love, then, and only then, may they like you.

Thank God for William Blake!

And thank William Blake for a very great deal of God!

There are five stages on the Mystic Road *(and no mystic yet has experienced them):* 1) Gaining a sense of the Divine; 2) The Emptying of Self; 3) Return to the Divine; 4) 'The Dark Night of the Soul' — torture of Self in separation from God; 5) The Total Identification with the All-Highest [or] 1) Birth (taste); 2) Hardship (smell); 3) Maturity (sight); 4) Decadence (hearing); 5) Transformation (touch).

> O
> Hell is not to exist.
> Heaven is creation. Most lives are dead.
> In man's deep middle is God.
> Trust the spirit. *Trust nothing else.*
> Let Aristotle watch his bears and foxes
> 'lick their whelps and cubs into shape.'
> That's all he's good for.
> No man is like any other man. Then struggle
> to your own freedom, rejecting as unsafe all
> others.
> The Redeemer — Fire burning fire —
> greater than Creator.
> Fixing-out the Thing Done Wrong.

Good is convention; Evil, energy; therefore,
Evil is the true Good.
No Law applies to all. Only God's. And His are
always lawless, breeding no serpents in the
heads of men.
To defile your Soul is to prove you none.
The Eagles of Prometheus bear the Cave
heavenward.
Fallen by Love: so rise!

> The poets speak for God when they let Him.
> Reason broke Desire's wing, revealing the Abyss
> — but Imagination has not seen it, having better
> eyes.
> O Flesh over Spirit equals Mud on the Stars.
> To imitate (— the Greeks —) is to paint a cab-
> bage because the Angel won't sit quite still
> enough.

Do as you want and what you want will make
everybody more beautiful.
Each thing that truly lives is sanctified.
You speak of self-restraint. Should the sun?
You are afraid to live. Then the thing you fear
is no factor in the case.
The only thing which should be suppressed is
suppression; should be killed is killing; should
be restrained denied retarded is restraint denial
etc., etc.
The only thing which can live is life. And
death, naturally, has nothing to do with dying.
The material world exists because *somebody*
went to the bother of imagining it.
Each really *new* one can do it better than the
last.
All the Great are unborn And don't insult
Those Noble Ones by not believing it.
TO FORGIVE IS TO UNDERSTAND.

ART IS GIVING.
    THE SAVED MUST SAVE THE REST!
To the North — the South, White country
To the East —
    I live! I breathe! I hate! I love!
To the West — that least region of the Spirit
To the South — here, the brain's little twitchings
To the
    O man is a flame!

Hurrah! Hurrah! HURRAH!
    Hurrah for William Blake!   □

A PATCHEN CHRONOLOGY

1911	Kenneth Frederick Patchen is born on December 13 in Niles, Ohio, to Wayne and Eva McQuade Patchen. He is the third child, preceeded by Eunice (born in 1902, died in a flu epidemic in 1913) and Hugh (born in 1903). The family is lower-middle-class economically, its members primarily coal miners and steel mill workers of Scotch and Irish ancestry.
1914	Majel Patchen is born on July 21.
1916	Kathleen Patchen is born; the family moves to Warren, Ohio, where Kenneth enters elementary school.
1920	The last child, Ruth, is born on January 22.
1923	Patchen starts a diary and writes his first poems.
1924	Enters East Junior High School in Warren.
1925	Kathleen is killed on her way to church by a car which jumps the sidewalk.
1926	Enters Warren G. Harding High School in Warren.
1926-1929	Active in many school activities including football, track, debate, school newspaper, Editor of the yearbook, *Echoes*, in 1929. His first publications, six poems in the school newspaper, *High School Life*, in 1928 and 1929.
1929	Spends the summer working in the steel mills. The family, which had become relatively prosperous, is now destitute.
1929-1930	Scholarship student at Alexander Meikeljohn's Experimental College at the University of Wisconsin.
1930	Attends Commonwealth College in Mena, Arkansas for several months. This marks the end of his formal education.

1930-1933	Travels around the United States and Canada taking odd jobs, including farm laborer, gardener, hiking shelter caretaker, and janitor. Spends several months in New York City.
1932	First regular publication, "Permanence," a sonnet, in the *New York Times*.
1933	Lives in Boston, where he is befriended by Conrad Aiken, John Wheelright, Malcolm Cowley, and others. At a party on Christmas Eve, he meets a young student, Miriam Oikemus, determining almost immediately to marry her.
1934	Works in a rubber plant near Boston, where he develops a severe sinus condition which necessitates an operation. Continues to correspond with Miriam; in the spring, they leave Boston for New York. Soon after, they go to Ohio, where they marry on June 28, a union which was to last Patchen's entire life. They move back to New York. Begins reviewing books for *New Republic*.
1935	Lives in New York City. Works on W.P.A. New York Guide. Receives a book contract from Random House. Goes to Rhinebeck, New York for several months to write *Before the Brave*.
1936	First book, *Before the Brave*, is published by Random House, reviewed by over fifty publications. Awarded Guggenheim Fellowship. Moves to Phoenix, Arizona, then Sante Fe, New Mexico.
1937	Moves to Los Angeles. Suffers disabling back injury.
1937-1938	Lives in Los Angeles, working on movie scripts. Works on W.P.A. California Guide.

1939 Spends time in Concord, Massachusetts. *First Will and Testament* published by James Laughlin's New Directions publishing company. Moves to Norfolk, Connecticut, where he and Miriam become, respectively, the accounting and shipping departments of New Directions.

1940 Moves to New York City. Begins to write *The Journal of Albion Moonlight*. Associates with Henry Miller, E.E. Cummings, Maxwell Bodenheim, and others.

1941 Unable to find a publisher who will risk bringing it out, the Patchens publish *The Journal of Albion Moonlight* by subscription. It is printed by Peter Beilenson at the Walpole Printing Office in Mount Vernon, New York, and "launched" at the Gotham Book Mart in New York City, whose owner, Frances Steloff, has purchased the entire trade edition of the book.

1942 *The Dark Kingdom*, the limited edition of which is the first of the "painted books," each carrying a different original work painted onto the cover by Patchen, is brought out by Harriss and Givens, their first and last book. *The Teeth of the Lion* is published in New Directions' "Poet of the Month" series. *The City Wears a Slouch Hat*, a radio play, is produced on Columbia Radio Workshop.

1943 Harper publishes *Cloth of the Tempest.*

1944 Visits Concord, Massachusetts. Receives Ohioana Award for *Cloth of the Tempest.*

1945 *Memoirs of a Shy Pornographer* (New Directions).

1946 Spends the summer in Mount Pleasant, then returns to New York City. *An Aston-*

ished Eye (Untide Press), *Outlaw of the Lowest Planet* (Grey Walls Press), *Panels for the Walls of Heaven* (Bern Porter), *The Selected Poems* (New Directions), *Sleepers Awake* (Padell), *They Keep Riding Down All the Time* (Padell), *Pictures of Life and of Death* (Padell) are all published. Padell also reprints *The Journal of Albion Moonlight* and other works.

1947   Moves to a house in Old Lyme, Connecticut, where he and Miriam remain for several years.

1948   *See You in the Morning* (Padell), Patchen's only "conventional" novel is published. *To Say If You Love Someone* (Decker) printed. *CCCLXXIV Poems* brought out by Padell, along with several reprints.

1950   First major operation on spine. Many benefit readings and concerts to raise money, through a fund headed by T.S. Eliot, Thornton Wilder, Archibald MacLeish, W.H. Auden, E.E. Cummings, Marianne Moore, William Carlos Williams, Edith Sitwell, and others.

1951   Moves to west coast for health reasons.

1952   Settles in San Francisco. *Orchards, Thrones, and Caravans* (The Print Workshop).

1953   *Fables and Other Little Tales* (Jargon).

1954   Receives Shelley Memorial Award. The City Lights Bookshop publishes *Poems of Humor and Protest* in their "Pocket Poets" series. *The Famous Boating Party* (New Directions).

1955   *Glory Never Guesses*, a silkscreen portfolio of picture-poems, is brought out.

1956   Moves to Palo Alto, California. Spends much

time at the Palo Alto Clinic, finally under-going a spinal fusion operation, which gives him some relief from pain for the first time in almost twenty years. The Patchens buy a house at 2340 Sierra Court in Palo Alto, the first place they have owned, and their final home. *Surprise for the Bagpipe Player*, another silkscreen portfolio, is produced.

1957   Begins the poetry-and-jazz movement, reading with jazz groups up and down the west coast until 1959. *Hurrah for Anything* (Jargon), *Kenneth Patchen Reads With the Chamber Jazz Sextet* (Cadence — recording), *When We Were Here Together* (New Directions), and *The Selected Poems, Enlarged Edition* (New Directions).

1958   *Poemscapes* (Jargon).

1959   A surgical "mishap" destroys the benefits of the 1956 operation, leaving Patchen in great pain, and rendering him almost completely bedridden for the rest of his life. *Don't Look Now*, his only full-length play, produced by the Troupe Theatre in Palo Alto. *Kenneth Patchen Reads His Selected Poems* (Folkways — recording), *Kenneth Patchen Reads With Jazz in Canada* (Folk-ways — recording).

1960   *Because It Is* (New Directions) and *The Love Poems* (City Lights). *The Moment*, a bound edition of *Glory Never Guesses* and *Surprise for the Bagpipe Player* is brought out.

1961   *Kenneth Patchen Reads His Love Poems* (Folkways — recording).

1966   *Hallelujah Anyway* (New Directions). *Doubleheader* (New Directions).

1967   Receives $10,000 award from the National

Foundation on the Arts and Humanities for "life-long contribution to American letters."

1968   *The Collected Poems of Kenneth Patchen* (New Directions), *But Even So* (New Directions), *Love & War Poems* (Whisper & Shout).

1970   *Aflame and Afun of Walking Faces* (New Directions), *There's Love All Day* (Hallmark).

1971   *Wonderings* (New Directions), *Tell You That I Love You* (Hallmark).

1972   Dies on January 8. *In Quest of Candlelighters* (New Directions), *Patchen's Funny Fables* (Greentree — recording), *The Journal of Albion Moonlight* (Folkways — recording).

1977   *Patchen's Lost Plays [Don't Look Now* and *The City Wears a Slouch Hat]* (Capra Press).

1977   *Kenneth Patchen: A Collection of Essays*, Richard Morgan, ed. (AMS Press)

1978   *Kenneth Patchen: An Annotated Descriptive Bibliography*, by Richard Morgan (Paul P. Appel)